10/30/17

TO GABE.
Thank you so much for
supporting my work !
.

Much Love,

Anxious

Anxious

A collection of Poems

By Shannell G. Griggs

I am the sister of two Kings!

This book is dedicated to my brother Hezekiah Griggs III who lost his life December 22, 2016. I love you Hezy. Thank you for being my big brother and showing me how to keep fighting for your dreams. When I lost you my life changed forever. You always told me to be strong and for you I will. Until we meet again. Rest in Peace

To my younger brother Ja'leel Boyce I dedicate this to you for being my strength. I remember crying at Hezy's funeral and you came and stood with me for hours telling me although I lost my big brother I still had you! I hope this inspires you to keep writing! You are the most amazing young man. I am so thankful and grateful to be your sister. The best gift mommy could have ever gave to me.

This is for all my siblings Shakeis Williams, Shafon Griggs, Kahliia Boyce. This is for us! We suffered great losses but we still fight every day to love more!

Table of Contents

A TRIBUTE TO HEZY 1

UNCHANGEABLE 6

THE DREAM 8

MY FIRST TIME 11

INTERNAL GENOCIDE 14

MY SOCIETY 16

THIS COLD WORLD 20

DEAR KOBE 23

FEELS LIKE SOMETHING'S MISSING 26

WHAT DOES IT MATTER 30

SOMETIMES 32

SHE WAS 34

99 AND HALF 36

HIM 38

TONIGHT 39

NOT A WORD 40

DON'T TOUCH MY SKIN 42

NOT READY 46

HOUSE SLAVE 47

G 49

ALL THAT I HAVE 50

ENOUGH 52

CLOUDS 53

FEAR IN THE POET 54

WHY HE TOOK A KNEE 56

COVERGIRL 60

ANXIOUS 61

ACKNOWLEDGMENTS 62

WHAT ARE YOU ANXIOUS ABOUT 63

Anxious

A tribute to Hezy

"Man and Lady"

Mustop sandwiches and koolaid that's what we ate that's what we

drank

We were inseparable and we once thought playdo was edible

Hezy remember the time you cooked on the real stove with my

fake food

Mommy came home smelled plastic burning the look on her face

we knew we were screwed

Hezy and Nell it's time for school. We would look at each other

act sick and pretend to swim back in the bed like it was a pool

We were always pretending our imaginations ran wild it was fun

We grew up lived a little but that bond that love I never forgot

where it all begun

F.A.C.E spells face and that's me I can still hear nick jr blasting on the TV

It was a busy world like Richard scary on 175 Sherman street

We watched Gullah island family matters we would sneak grandads snacks we would never tell

Always getting into a little trouble like Zac but was never saved by the bell

We made fish with pepper had toilet paper parties we were true rock stars

We used mommy's old records and crates like the little rascals we made our own race cars

It was a time when all we had was each other my little big brother

On the playground being your protector fighting back the bullies

Telling whoever would listen if you want my brother, first you have to get through me

Back then I was a little tougher than you I played a little harder

And then to teach you how to be a man you went down south to be with our father

I remember missing you like crazy and all I wanted was to be

there with you

So I wished on a couple of stars and closed my eyes really tight

and my wish came true

We had fun down there we played house made fake money with

grandpas printer

We played restaurant I was the waitress and you were the

businessman as I served you dinner

Man Hezy remember those good memories we never did get that

house tree

We ate lots of candies told a lot of jokes we got older you learned

new things and tried to teach me the ropes

I remember a time when all we had was each other my little big

brother

I don't want to fast forward I know what's going to happen I know you're going to leave

So I'll live back in these times at least until I'm strong enough to

believe

To accept the fact that you are gone you died on December 22nd

of 2016 the worst day of my life

No more pretending the pain is so deep feels like my heart was

cut in half with a knife

We were inseparable Hezy we really thought playdo was edible

Mustop sandwiches and koolaid is what we ate and drank

My best friend my beautiful brother you will never be replaced

there will never be another

Hezekiah Griggs III a magnificent being

I will forever cherish your memory

One day we will meet again and everything won't be what it

seems

For now I'll wait to speak to you in my dreams

There are so many other stories I could tell but my emotions are raging and I just want to yell

Hezy don't leave please come back to me but that's me being

selfish something I don't want to be

You have to go home and Rest In Peace

Rest well my brother and let all your problems release

It's hard to say goodbye when I look in the mirror I see you

through my eyes

Wish we had more time in my heart I'll hold you

you will forever be mine

My big brother my other half the man to my lady the mutt to my

Jeff

Just want to pour my pain in this poem until I have nothing left

There was a time when all we had was each other I love you

Hezy aka my big brother

Hezekiah Griggs III Rest in Peace

Unchangeable

I am who I am and I'm not going to change

I am who I am and I will remain the same

You always try and change me into something I'm not

And quite frankly it must stop

You can either love me or leave but don't try and break me

I'm tired of living a lie

I'm tired of asking God why

Why you just can't love me for the person I was made into

Always telling me what I should do

How I should wear my hair and the clothes that I wear

But I'm here to tell you that I really don't care

I don't care if you don't like me

I don't care if you try and fight me

7

I don't care if you try to break me down

And I don't care if you scorn my name all around town

Because for too long I was made to believe you was right for me

For too long I was made to believe you was who I wanted to be

I'm so glad that I see things clearer and I'm so glad I've been

drawn nearer

Nearer to self-respect, nearer to self-esteem,

Nearer to everything I should have been loved about me

You covered my eyes and filled them with so much hate

It was my fault because I was weak which made me easy bait

But thank God I finally found where I stand, with my head held

high looking over this land

So forget you negativity and yea it's like that

Go away and I pray that you never come back!

The Dream

When will we stop dreaming the dream and live the dream

So many people wait around for a change to come and grab their

hand

They subject themselves to let people make them fall when they

can be sturdy and stand

Stand up for life's goals, dreams, and ambitions

I can't let that happen to me because I'm God's child and blessed

Christian

I stand up for what I believe in even if I stand alone

I speak from my heart purity from my dome

The pride of the people the fight never stops

Proving to Webster that blacks are human whether he wants to

believe it or not

So, when will we stop dreaming the dream and live the dream

So many greats paved the way for you and me

Not just blacks they stood for human integrity

But some of us walk around like that means nothing

Like our ancestors died for nothing

So I ask, when will we stop dreaming the dream and live the

dream

Not even a half a century ago my people couldn't go into a nice

restaurant to sit down and eat

They were treated like savages a worthless piece of meat

Smart enough to get through any situation even though they

never had the proper education

But with determination, dedication, and self-inspiration

We made it thus far but still a long way to go

But one question troubles my mind and I must know

Just when will we stop dreaming the dream and become the

dream

Consider this your wakeup call because it's long past due

Wake up, are still dreaming because I'm talking to you

My First Time

Last night was so amazing how you made love to me

You kept me up all night releasing me further into my ecstasy

Our intimacy was immediately filled with passionate foods for

thought

It was the heart in my head you so quickly not stole but bought

Yea you kept me up all night making love to my brain

My mind climaxed to every intellect word you obtained

You see I, lost my brain virginity to you and you so well deserved

it

It felt so good to know someone was finally worth it

Don't worry wrap it up we had safe thoughts

We strapped up with Webster and backed up with oxfords divinities

So, we wouldn't have to worry about the dreadful std of a brain attack

Or the dreadful pregnancy

To let in another intellect ...

3's a party and I'm not trying to get my heart, I mean mind broken again

So yea you kept me up all night

Penetrating my thoughts deeper and deeper with each stroke of wisdom you explored

Your exploration was a success and you have earned yourself a reward

How you fore played with a brain tease that had me in a frenzy

Damn I went crazy

Uumm, how you massage that book

13

How you pull each page behind the other

How you use your index finger to indent knowledge into me

brother

You got me I said you have me

I want you true I'm like sperm I'll fight just to be embedded in you

While on my knees giving ultimate pleasure but only to pray for

you

As you eat my ignorance and fill me with your intelligence

What a brave heart I lack your soul

You make me here

You make me whole

My first time

Internal Genocide

They told her "You will never amount to anything and be nothing"

So, she went out in the streets looking for something

She turned on the block and saw a man on a corner

And gave her life away cause nobody warned her

She wore blisters on her feet because her heels were too high

It was clear if you saw her that sex you can buy

He told her what to do so you can say she was robotic with no

human attributes she was dehumanized and forgot it

She had no mental stability so you can say she had no brain

So, the AID and low white blood cells took up all the pain

The pain she was carrying from the hurt on her heart

So, God came from the heavens and took her soul from that part

She would still be alive if she didn't listen to what they said and

could laugh and nibble on all the lies that they fed

Her life was like a movie a tape steady rolling, but she always let

those people change the good that was showing

Now, what if she became that actress doctor lawyer she so

wanted to be?

Proving the laws of people's nature wrong which is herself

sometimes me even we

I've closed so many doors in my because of what people said I

couldn't do and if they were in this room right now all I want to do

is say F you!

That woman in the story could be so many young ladies that "you

aint ish" was instilled in them since babies

So, the next time I let someone change my mind because of their

percent's and fractions

It'll be my fault I didn't make it because I let someone's words

affect my actions.

My society

As gas prices go up so do crack heads demands

No more ten cents these people want dollar bills in their hands

and as this drug affected infected never to be corrected directed

his needs to me

Is when I noticed something that begin to bother me

Really it disturbed me like the time I went to an all-black school

and learned nothing for Black history because the administration

thought that Dr. King and Malcolm X was enough history or

maybe Harriet Tubman because she revolved around slavery

but that was high school years

As I walk down the streets of my society I see two young girls

crying saying to their mothers I'm hungry

and what mattered most was neither mother seemed to be able to

stop this tragedy

A tragedy of a vicious cycle that seems to never end when

sixteen-year-old children are bearing potential fifteen-year-old

children who will end up having a baby, and there's no one there

to save them so there's no one there to tame them

So, my heart begins to feel like the time my mom dated this guy

who toyed and played with the pump of her heart never caring for

her from the start but "WE" got over it dad

 but that was childhood years and I went to counseling for that

As I walk deeper in the streets of my society I see a grown man

try to holler at this young lady

her name was Crystal but he persisted to call her baby and she

liked it

 I mean all she did was laugh and giggle as he told her ass was

big and how he probably could and would work the middle

The middle of her innocence the middle of her heart basically

tearing this whole girl mind and body apart

but this is my society crying out for me

I hear no hearts because all is broken

because every mom is crying

News just came in her little boy is dying

Retrospect...

"at *the tender age of six he was diagnosed with the doctors death*

called cancer and in one year Dr. L said he would breathe his last

breath that one year became 12 and he lived to see 18 no more

chemo football genius can you believe so why is his mom crying

he's a cancer survivor thankfully unlike cancer guns have no

chemo in my society"

Wow back to now this kid survived reality but got killed because

of stupidity a problem that shouldn't be

Guns are cancer metaphorically

And stuff like this is evident in my society

Vicious cycles seem to never stop

Next week yellow tape through my whole block

Because that one baby neglected

Teen pregnancy

Street poverty

Hey Miss, can I have a dollar is all you hear in my society

This Cold World

This world is filled with so much hatred and there's no one to

blame cause,

Every time I turn on the news it's always the same and it's really

ashame

There's never anything good especially in my neck of the woods

Mothers, fathers, and children are steady crying

cause their loved ones are steady dying

Why must we kill each other?

Why must we fight?

It's got so bad they got me afraid to be outside at night

Nowadays it's hard to see eighteen, even though you are still a

teen

This world ain't giving no breaks

Look, they don't care about your dreams and what you wish to be

cause they tainted with stupidity so they just can't see

"See what", I hear them say

The lives that you selfishly take each day

That was someone's father, no he can't come back now I hear

you saying how you wish you never bothered

And that was someone's son, no he can't come back cause you

already put a bullet in that one

That was someone's daughter I hear you crying saying how you

wish your bullet never caught her

But why you had to take their mother? do you know how much

her family really loved her?

Would you wake up now and change this cold cold world

Just think if that was your little boy or girl lying there lifeless

bloody on the ground it's 9 o'clock and her family is hoping and

praying she'll be found, but when they get there it's too late cause she's already dead and the next morning this is how the paper read,

"Nine year old girl body found slain, she's leaves a mother father and two siblings who are all facing a lot of pain, autopsy says she was shot in the heart, now this leaves her parents torn apart, they say the killer was aiming for someone else but it didn't happen that way

her funeral will be held at Beaks Funeral Home down by the bay"

I hope you hear this story and start to get some sense because innocent people are dying because of your ignorance
Take heed and stop the violence and change this cold world
So, we won't hear on the news about another little boy or girl!

Dear Kobe

You are

"Kobe Bryant the slam dunk giant

Number one riant

Played out the kid son don't try it"

I'm going to miss seeing you fly jump and conquer all on that

court

Shooting 3's dunking playing amazing basketball defining the true

meaning of the sport

What's next for you? What else will you amaze us with in this

time?

Because since you are leaving the game I don't what I'm going to

do with mine

When I chose to love a great athlete I knew you were the one to

believe in

Everything you accomplished for the NBA proving the non-

believers wrong time and time again

The Lakers all-time leading scorer, back to back rings man you

did your thing

Twenty years, five championships, don't even have to mention

facts they will remain the same

I was honored to see you play all these years

Knowing the "black mamba" will play no more brings me to tears

You are so amazing I named my nephew after you

If God would have blessed me with a son 1st I would have named

him Kobe too

Just because your name means greatness and you have proven

that throughout my life

I wish nothing but peace joy and happiness for you, your children

and your wife

You are

"Kobe Bryant the slam dunk giant

Number one riant

Played out the kid son don't try it"

Sincerely a respectful fan Shannell

Feels Like

Something's

Missing

I feel like I'm missing something

Maybe it's the virginity that was taken away from me

Loud cries turned to silent tears first it was yes then no, had to

learn to forgive him over the years

I feel like I'm missing something

Maybe it's my honesty covered by lies recovered by fake truth so

you couldn't notice the pain in my eyes

I feel like I'm missing something

Maybe it's the fulfillment of food from the hungry little girl dying inside me

Seems as if my past keeps haunting me

I feel like I'm missing something

Maybe it was the blood that was supposed to circulate through my body at fifteen that gushed out my nose and eyes to the ground

All because some girls that I didn't fit in with searched for a thug within in me that couldn't be found

I feel like I'm missing something

Maybe it was the love sucked out of me by a man who used me made me believe I was worthless like a slave and abused me, I couldn't be free

I feel like I'm missing something

Maybe it's the bullet that was supposed to be in my head after he put a gun to it threatening me not to leave or me being dumb to believe he that because he loved me

I feel like I'm missing something

Maybe it's my sanity I gave away because society hurt me and

made me feel my life should go away

It feels like I'm missing something

Maybe it's the friendship that I was supposed to get from so called

friends, but when times get different and I can't give no more

that's when friendship ends

It feels like I'm missing something

Maybe it's my heart that I've given away so many times and never

got back, so I'm left with pieces and it feels at times I'll have a

heart attack

It feels like I'm missing something

Maybe it's the victories I couldn't see the battles I didn't win and

all the fear inside that I always try to defend

It feels like I'm missing something

Maybe it's the sleepless nights up thinking about what I should've

done, all the struggles and trials I've should've won

It feels like I'm missing something

29

Maybe it's just me not being who I'm supposed to be dying and

living at the same time

Maybe I'm missing something and this go around it won't be my

mind

It feels like I'm missing something

One second, let me go get it back

Shannell

What does it matter

Hands up or hands down what does it matter

Peaceful or aggressive what does it matter

Good man bad man what does it matter

Living old or dying young what does it matter

Broken tail light or missed signal what does it matter

Hands up or hands down what does it matter

Hoodie or button down what does it matter

Gun on gun off what does it matter

Going in or coming out the store what does it matter

Standing or kneeling what does it matter

Late nights early mornings what does it matter

The color of skin in the blue suit what does it matter

Big signs and marching what does it matter

Standing for your beliefs what does it matter

Hands up hands down what does it matter

Hands up hands down

What does it matter

Black and white

What does it matter

Black and white

It matters

What matters?

Sometimes

Sometimes you have to be prepared to take on unfortunate life events

Sometimes you have to deal with the unimaginable

Sometimes you have to fight at your weakest

Sometimes you have to accept loves deceit

Sometimes you have to look love in the eye and say I hate you

Sometimes you have to give love another chance

Sometimes you have to forgive the hurt

Sometimes you have to live with the pain

Sometimes you have to move forward and never look back

Sometimes you have to look back to see where you came from

Sometimes life makes no sense

33

Sometimes you'll just feel like shit

Sometimes you have to make it

Sometimes you have to believe things you don't want to

Sometimes...

She Was

She was a beautiful person or at least she tried to be

She became whoever someone wanted her to be to make them happy

She was destructive in her mind and sad to heart

She was strong for others and gave weakness to herself

She was loving and kind

She was the bad apple but she was also the blossoming flower

She was a doormat in front of the busy building

She gave all to living and fantasized with the dead

35

She was envious of one's death sad for her soul

She tried to see the bigger picture but the lens was too small

She was a beautiful song played for the kings and queens

She was here and she tried her best to live...

She was

99 and half years

She is beauty from a place we only can desire

She is courage and with her love she ignites a fire

A fire with no harm to life but to warm the hearts of those on a cold

lonely night

She is rich in time and wise beyond years

She is the prayer warrior to block all our fears

Her soul will continue to do the work of God

She is now our angel because on earth she's done her job

Like Jesus she drew us nearer to our heavenly father and destiny

She taught us good thoughts and always instilled the best in we

Her voice and heartbeat played the sweetest song

God blessed us with her to have for 99 and half years long

Her cup never runneth over the straw couldn't break her back

She survived so much over the years she conquered every attack

Grandma Scott your strength is something we all wish to have a piece
of

Go home job well done rest in peace our love

Thank you for your life your time your talks your strength and your love

Rest in peace and watch down on us from heaven above

We can still feel your heartbeat the sweetest melody in our song

God, thank you for letting us have grandma Scott for 99 and a half years
long

HIM

He hides from life so he uses the pipe

He can't look at himself he has been ran over

Don't want to deal with the presence so has never been sober

He had some beautiful children but they can't call him dad

He knows he's not a father now tell me that's sad

Intelligent he is and he knows his books

But to addicted to the streets they got him hooked

He hides from life he hides from me

I wish he would bother because I could use a father

Dad I never had

Tonight

Lay here with me just for the night

Pleasure is pleasure

Infect me with your poison

Give it to me

I said I want it yes now

I need it now I can't wait any longer

Pass me the remote to the television

Please my show is about to go off damn

Quick

Not A Word

The cotton pickers would love to hear this

The slaved ones will rejoice to hear this

The men in black would love to feel this

I am the nigger beaten raped and spit on hung from a tree

The mother whose milk was stolen in the breast sucked out from my

babies

The men forced to kneel on knees to perform acts to mankind

Forced to such touch lick feel the white poison soon to find

I am the negro anthem hummed in disparaged white pastures of hatred

Genocidal plantations death cometh in the morning if master hears me

say this

They called me nigger to belittle me they called me nigger to

dehumanize me

So, do you really want to abolish my bravery your history?

Is this what I've left as my memory?

Being a nigger is something I fault not be

My pain is deeply rooted in the fact that I was never free

Let my voice be the reason and my past be the trigger my people today

you could not possibly be a nigger

For my ancestors

Don't touch my skin

Don't touch skin.

You don't know what I've been through.

You don't know the black I have to defend.

You don't know the struggle of being black and not fitting in.

So don't talk about my color, so what if I don't get much tan in the summer.

What is for my melanin ain't strong enough?

Not enough roots.

My berry ain't sweet enough?

sour juice.

Don't touch my skin.

When I battle loneliness and confusion within.

Being told by my people I don't belong.

Can't lift my voice and sing cause that's not my song.

Don't talk about my color being light ain't always right.

Wanting to be darker to feel connected to complexion.

Kicked out and forced to be in the not dark enough or light

enough section.

Don't talk to me.

Not if you're going to question my nationality

His dream was for me too

the ones who look like me marched with you.

They were sprayed too, their bodies were scarred , first black then

blue .

They looked for rescue, they still have credit that's due. My

pigment is black too.

Don't touch my skin not if your not going to acknowledge where I've been.

Feeling lost in the world of color that was my ancestors master sin.

Can you accept me? As part of your history

Can you look past my skin and see the black within?

Or will you continue to sigh and not say high because your skin is darker than mine.

Why are we divided it's 2000 something anyway our ancestors already paved the way.

So, we don't have to argue about who would have been in the house or field anymore.

My black your black our black is beautiful and from this day forward it won't be ignored.

45

So, don't touch my skin, you'll never understand the black I have to defend.

Thank you to Solange Knowles for making an incredible inspirational album. Credit to "Don't touch my hair" off her "Seat at the table" album.

Not Ready

If you weren't ready why are you even here.

You knew who I was why were you even there.

I'll be who I am till my repass most likely

So, if you're not ready I recommend you leave quietly.

I've tried all possibilities and reasons to try and figure out what

was wrong with me

I come up empty

I know one thing I'm young & in charge and life moves on whether

you're here or not my life will be steady.

Baby I love you but you just not ready.

House slave

They say I'm the house nigga

The color of my skin makes things this way

I'm light-skinned so that means I'm not black enough to really be a

part of black society today

They say I would have been the house slave and I know nothing

about the black struggle through these times

I'm just in the house feet kicked sipping lemonade with cool air

just master and I

House slave field slave what was the difference

Inside outside still enslaved there is no difference

but I'm the house Nigga, I'm in the house Nigga,

I'm still a nigga to them light-skinned people got lynched to Nigga

Not me but she was a house slave that's true

48

that doesn't mean things were all that beautiful

while the "dark ones are outside" singing finding ways to escape

she's in the house is getting beaten, raped by master and use a

sex slave

So. come on in the house and see if you could make it

being under masters nose all day beaten if you're not perfect

As an entire race, we were dehumanized regardless of the house

or field we were beaten in

light, black, brown still black still suppressed still hurt still hung still

on genocidal plantations,

but what do I know I'm just a house slave and the color of my

skin makes life easy

I guess the house slave has nothing to do with our black history

G

The definition of love is how I feel about you.

Telling you I love you over and over is pointless because truth is

my love for you will never be justified by laws of nature it's too off

radar

My heart your passion my heart your laughter my heart your love

they are all intertwined through a love that will never be defined

an over achieved feeling that can't be handled in this time

Over beaming always caring our hearts beating together as one

A new definition of love has just begun.

To Givonni Butler

All that I have

I only have my heart

I only have my mind body and soul

I'm not selfish I love to share with you

Loving someone easy but finding someone to love you is harder

to discover

I have to constantly prove my love over and over makes me

wonder if I cracked the case if I have solved the puzzle and broke

through concrete to get to the light

You constantly wonder what do they feel? Am I beauty to them?

Am I embedded in their thoughts so much that I am seen in

dreams?

All that I have is my heart but all that I want is yours

I rather have yours because I know no one has it

51

I know you haven't used it often or let many people abuse it

I want to trade my heart in for yours make my love payments on

time until it's time for me to pay it off

Heart fax came back good love beats are working fine and it's a

clean non-Salvaged heart

hoping one day that's what I'll have

All that I have is my heart all that I want is yours

Inspired by Singer Teedra Moses

Thank you for great music

Enough

You can give a person so much and still that isn't enough

sometimes I want to leave but I'm just not strong enough

When will I say, I tried I failed enough is enough

when will I wake up to clear skies and sunny days

When happiness becomes enough

Can I have a heart a soul a love a body that will be for me not too

much but just enough

My body says I don't have enough not enough to laugh not

enough to smile

I tried to cry no tears came out because I didn't have enough

But I had enough

Enough of want I don't need

enough just enough to leave .. enough

Clouds

Blue skies and white clouds is all I see

true winds and dark nights is all I need

chasing clouds is like trying to catch a balloon after it's been let go

Somewhat impossible

clouds and life are so similar

 Life is living like clouds are there to give us hope

something seen not felt

Clouds...

The fear in the poet

So much paper and afraid to pick up the pen.

To finally unlock his story within.

His fear of not saying what is right in his mind.

Allowing his fear to block his true destiny he needs to find.

Powerful thoughts locked away in his head.

Every night battling his words so sleep never finds his bed.

What he doesn't know is someone needs to be saved by his words.

So maybe they can be set free like the story of the caged birds.

His lover waits for the day she'll hear his words through her ears.

Watching over him praying that he'll find the courage to write after all these years

55

I feel him fighting to see the creation that he has yet to create.

Trying to leave all fear behind a jail in his thoughts fighting to

escape.

When the time comes for him we will know it.

Because there will be a change in this world and no more fear in

the poet.

Why he took a knee

All because he kneeled doesn't mean he doesn't love his country.

And all because he kneeled and I'm black doesn't mean he's speaking for me.

But because all people do in this country is try to divide us is the reason I'm going to be with him and speak about this injustice .

So, let me get this straight kneeling for the national anthem makes him an ingrate?

And tell me exactly what is it that he's ungrateful for?

They scream stand up have respect this is what they implore

He loves his country and that's why he's here.

All because he took a knee shouldn't mean you have to fear

Don't be afraid of a statement to make a change you not

understanding his why knowing what's going on is strange.

It's like you choose to see what you want to see

quick to say you're not the bad guy but can't respect his decision

to take a knee.

He didn't say F America and forget about the troops

he shouldn't be compared to the kkk and other racist groups.

Organizations who have committed hate crimes against a specific

race.

He and those who kneeled with him should not be categorized but

embraced

All because he kneeled doesn't mean he doesn't love his country

What that flag and the anthem mean a knee could never erase.

What our ancestors fought for the love and commitment a knee

could never replace.

To even consider one's love because of a knee is a disgrace.

Of course, he loves his country his ancestors died here for you

and me

there is probably still DNA on the sidewalks or limbs from the

trees where his people were beaten and hung from then cut and

knocked to their knees.

Just think for a minute and open your eyes and see

See what like before I keep hearing them say.

The fact that our ancestors died for us so we wouldn't have to

pay,

Pay for your insecurities and lack of respect for who we are you

don't want nothing if you had the power you would block the

night's sky so we couldn't wish on a star

Yes, not just blacks but there were others who fought for the flag

and anthem to have its meaning,

and that shouldn't make you feel his peaceful protest is demeaning.

Maybe to him the piece his people our people contributed to the flag and anthem don't get the appreciation earned, and so the truth in those stripes and the colors who protected it was never learned

A man takes a knee in life to show respect his future wife.

They kneel to propose an offer of life together in trust.

So, maybe he took the knee to re-engage so that America can be re-consider how to treat us.

You see it as disrespect I see it as a way to reconnect

So, stop questioning his love for his country and let him be free maybe you should think and recommit yourself and finally take a knee

Cover girl

I let those with blind eyes take beauty away from me

I let my imperfections and insecurities dictate my pretty

I let the magazines images and thoughts of what "they like"

decide how I would feel about myself

I thought cover girls didn't cry I thought they didn't need any help

I allowed those girls he cheated with make me feel I didn't look

right.

And because he didn't tell me or show me I was beautiful on the

regular, I kept out his sight

I didn't know beauty could be me if my granny and grandma didn't

tell me

Thought they were being kind because I was theirs

Thought they were just telling me what I deserved

I thought cover girls didn't cry I thought they didn't need any help

But I cry and you cry…

Anxious

I am ready for change

Ready to wake up and fix the mistakes of yesterday

I am trying to discover my true potential

I want to forgive the ones who hurt me

But I am afraid my forgiveness will get them off the hook too easy

I want to live my dreams

I can't wait

I am ready for change

I like this pain

I like this feeling

I want to be happy but I am comfortable with sorrow

I toss and turn and my heart over beats

I will wait until my time comes

I will be content

I will still worry

Patiently Anxious

Anxious but Patient

Still Anxious

Anxious…

Acknowledgments

I just want to say thank you to everyone who supports me. To everyone who purchased my first book. To all the people who invited me to perform and cheered for me along the way. All the stages I was honored to stand on even if mistakes were made I still got an over whelming applause. From the bottom of my heart. Thank you!

Love always, Shannell Gloria Griggs

What are you

anxious about?

WRITE

DRAW

CREATE

DREAM

This is your 30-day guide to be free and live through your art and creativity. Enjoy!

64

Day 1

65

Day 2

Day 3

Day 4

68

Day 5

69

Day 6

70

Day 7

Day 8

Day 9

73

Day 10

Day 11

75

Day 12

76

Day 13

77

Day 14

78

Day 15

79

Day 16

80

Day 17

Day 18

Day 19

Day 20

84

Day 21

85

Day 22

86

Day 23

87

Day 24

88

Day 25

Day 26

Day 27

Day 28

Day 29

Day 30

Anxious